Other Giftbooks by Exley:
The Kiss   When Love is Forever
The Wicked Little Book of Quotes   The Glory of Love

Published simultaneously in 1996 by Exley Publications in Great Britain,
and Exley Giftbooks in the USA.

12 11 10 9 8 7 6 5 4 3

Copyright © Helen Exley 1996

Edited and pictures selected by Helen Exley.
Picture research by Image Select, London.
Typeset by Delta, Watford
Printed and bound in China

Exley Publications Ltd, 16 Chalk Hill, Watford, Herts WD1 4BN, UK.
Exley Giftbooks, 232 Madison Avenue, Suite 1206, New York, NY 10016, USA.

Passion

*Quotations
on the
consuming desire
of great love*

A Helen Exley Giftbook

EXLEY
NEW YORK • WATFORD, UK

I love you soulfully and bodyfully, properly and improperly, every way that a woman can be loved.

GEORGE BERNARD SHAW (1856-1950), TO ELLEN TERRY

Love isn't decent. Love is glorious and shameless.

ELIZABETH VON ARNIM (1866-1941), FROM "LOVE"

Adèle, are you aware that the word "passion" means "suffering"? And do you believe, in all honesty, that there is any suffering in these love affairs of commen men, which are apparently so turbulent, but in fact so insipid? No, immortal love is eternal, because the being which experiences it is immortal. It is our souls which love and not our bodies.

VICTOR HUGO (1802-1885), TO ADELE FOUCHER

*L*ike a fierce wind roaring high up
in the bare branches of trees, a
wave of passion came over me,
aimless but surging.... I suppose
it's lust but it's awful and holy
like thunder and lightning and
the wind.

JOANNA FIELD

He had robbed the body of its
taint, the world's taunts of their
sting; he had shown her the
holiness of direct desire.

E.M. FORSTER (1879-1970)

... the life and love of the body
is a noble thing, against which
the intellect and the spirit need
not wage war.

MICHELE ROBERTS

Opening

He knew that when he kissed this
girl, his mind would never romp
again like the mind of God.... Then
he kissed her. At his lips' touch she
blossomed for him like a flower and
the incarnation was complete.

F. SCOTT FITZGERALD (1896-1940),
FROM *"THE GREAT GATSBY"*

He came to me with the most
wonderful tenderness. He was afraid
and I was afraid, but there it was,
that openness: he was as delicate
and fragile and beautiful as a
flower, the blossom trembling in
full bloom....

VICTORIA FREEMAN

I gave thee what could not be heard,

What had not been given before;

The beat of my heart I gave....

EDITH M. THOMAS (1854-1925)

*L*ove, my heart longs day and night for the meeting with you – for the meeting that is like all-devouring death.

Sweep me away like a storm; take everything I have; break open my sleep and plunder my dreams....

Rob me of my world.

In that devastation, in the utter nakedness of spirit, let us become one in beauty.

RABINDRANATH TAGORE,
FROM *"THE GARDENER"*

... COME APART
IN YOUR HANDS
LIKE PIECES OF A VAST
AND UNSOLVED PUZZLE.

LINDA PASTAN, b. 1932

HERE UNDER THE SHOCK OF LOVE, I AM OPEN
TO YOU....

MAY SARTON, b. 1912

WHERE DESIRE DOTH BEAR THE SWAY,
THE HEART MUST RULE, THE HEAD OBEY.

ANONYMOUS

...if you can't come into the room without my feeling all over me a ripple of flame, & if, wherever you touch me, a heart beats under your touch, & if, when you hold me, & I don't speak, it's because all the words in me seem to have become throbbing pulses, & all my thoughts are a great golden blur....

EDITH WHARTON (1862-1937),
TO W. MORTON FULLERTON

*A*S SOON AS THE SUN

HIDES BEHIND THE VERDANT MOUNTAINS,

THEN JET-BLACK

NIGHT WILL COME.

SMILING RESPLENDENTLY

LIKE THE MORNING SUN,

WITH YOUR ARMS

WHITE AS ROPE OF TAKU FIBRES,

YOU WILL EMBRACE

MY BREAST THRILLING WITH YOUTH,

SOFT AS THE LIGHT SNOW;

WE SHALL EMBRACE AND ENTWINE OUR BODIES.

YOUR JEWEL-LIKE HANDS

WILL TWINE WITH MINE,

AND, YOUR LEGS OUTSTRETCHED,

YOU WILL LIE AND SLEEP...

PRINCESS NUNAKAWA,
FROM ANCIENT MYTHOLOGICAL WRITING

I have decked my bed with
coverings of tapestry, with carved works, with fine
linen of Egypt. I have perfumed my bed with
myrrh, aloes and cinammon.
Come, let us take our fill of love until the morning.

PROVERBS

I will allow only
My lord to possess my sacred
Lotus pond, and every night
You can make blossom in me
Flowers of fire.

HUANG O (1498-1569)
FROM "THE ORCHID BOAT"

Awake, O north wind; and come, thou south; blow
upon my garden, that the spices thereof may flow
out. Let my beloved come into his garden, and eat
his pleasant fruits.

SONG OF SOLOMON

Passion

Passion never reasons.

COMTESSE DU BARRY (1746-1793)

*Passion is not so much an emotion as a
destiny. What choice have I in the face of
this wind but to put up my sail and
rest my oars?*

JEANETTE WINTERSON, b. 1959

*The only sin passion can commit
is to be joyless.*

DOROTHY SAYERS (1893-1957)

*It is the passion that is in the kiss that gives
to it its sweetness; it is the affection in a
kiss that sanctifies it.*

CHRISTIAN NESTELL BOVÉE

... THE FURIOUS STORM THROUGH ME

CAREERING — I PASSIONATELY TREMBLING;

THE OATH OF THE INSEPARABLENESS OF TWO

TOGETHER — OF THE WOMAN THAT LOVES ME,

AND WHOM I LOVE MORE THAN MY LIFE

— THAT OATH SWEARING;

(O I WILLINGLY STAKE ALL, FOR YOU!

O LET ME BE LOST, IF IT MUST BE SO!

O YOU AND I — WHAT IS IT TO US WHAT

THE REST DO OR THINK?

WHAT IS ALL ELSE TO US? ONLY THAT WE

ENJOY EACH OTHER, AND EXHAUST EACH OTHER,

IF IT MUST BE SO....

WALT WHITMAN (1819-1891),
FROM *"FROM PENT-UP, ACHING RIVERS"*

She remembered the dreamlike sequence of clothes coming off and the two of them naked in bed. She remembered how he held himself just above her and moved his chest slowly against her belly and across her breasts. How he did this again and again, like some animal courting rite in an old zoology text. As he moved over her, he alternately kissed her lips or ears or ran his tongue along her neck, licking her as some fine leopard might do in long grass out on the veld.

He was an animal. A graceful, hard,

male animal who did nothing overtly to

dominate her yet dominated her completely,

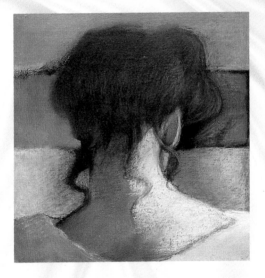

in the exact way she wanted that to happen

at this moment.

ROBERT JAMES WALLER,
FROM *"THE BRIDGES OF MADISON COUNTY"*

Only he felt he could no more dissemble
And kissed her, mouth to mouth, all in a tremble.

LEIGH HUNT (1784-1859), FROM "STORY OF RIMINI"

Upon that ground her robe was spread,
And on that robe was lain my head;
Into its folds, burningly yearning.
My lips went, pouring kisses, till
I shook with ecstasy.

EBENEZER JONES (1820-1860), FROM "EMILY"

... You touched my life.

My life reaches the skin, moves

   under your smile,

And your throat and your shoulders

   and your face and your thighs

Flash.

... The spaces of the body

Are suddenly limitless....

MURIEL RUKEYSER (1913-1980)

Electric

He glared at her a moment through the dusk, and the next instant she felt his arms about her and his lips on her own lips. His kiss was like white lightning, a flash that spread, and spread again, and stayed.

HENRY JAMES (1843-1916),
FROM *"THE PORTRAIT OF A LADY"*

... 7he curve of your breast is like the curve

of a wave: look, held, caught, each instant

caught, the wave tipping over and we

in our bower,

the two of us sheltered, my hands on

your thighs,

your body, your back, my mouth on

your mouth

and in the hollows of your jaws and your head

nuzzling my breasts. And the wave above us is

folding over now, folding and laughing.

   Will you

take to the sea, my darling? Will you let me

   caress you?

The tips of your feet, your legs, your sex?

Will you let my tongue caress you? Will you

lie in my arms? Will you rest? And if the sun

is too strong, should burn too much, will you

walk with me to where the light is more calm

and be in me where the seas heave and are

serene and heave again and are themselves?

SUNITI NAMJOSHI, b.1941

*L*ove has no other desire but to fulfil itself.

But if you love and must needs have desires,
    let these be your desires:

To melt and be like a running brook that
    sings its melody to the night.

To know the pain of too much tenderness.

To be wounded by your own understanding
    of love;

And to bleed willingly and joyfully.

To wake at dawn with a winged heart and
    give thanks for another day of loving;

To rest at the noon hour and meditate love's
    ecstasy;

To return home at eventide with gratitude;

And then to sleep with a prayer for the
    beloved in your heart and a song of
    praise upon your lips.

KAHLIL GIBRAN (1883-1931), FROM *"THE PROPHET"*

your slightest look easily will

unclose me

though i have closed myself as

fingers,

you open always petal by petal

myself as Spring opens

(touching skilfully, mysteriously)her

first rose

E.E. CUMMINGS (1864-1962),
FROM "SOMEWHERE I HAVE NEVER TRAVELLED,
GLADLY BEYOND"

And her lips opened amorously, and said—

I wist not what, saving one word – Delight.

And all her face was honey to my mouth,

And all her body pasture to mine eyes;

The long lithe arms and hotter hands than fire

The quivering flanks, hair smelling of the south,

The bright light feet, the splendid supple thighs

And glittering eyelids of my soul's desire.

ALGERNON CHARLES SWINBURNE (1837-1909),
FROM *"LOVE AND SLEEP"*

I will cover you with love when next I see you, with caresses, with ecstasy. I want to gorge you with all the joys of the flesh, so that you faint and die. I want you to be amazed by me, and to confess to yourself that you had never even dreamed of such transports.... When you are old I want you to recall those few hours, I want your dry bones to quiver with joy when you think of them.

GUSTAVE FLAUBERT (1821-1880), TO LOUISE COLET

I belong to you! We're going to have a week such as we never dreamt yet. "The thermometer will burst." I want to feel again the violent thumping inside of me, the rushing, burning blood, the slow, caressing rhythm and the sudden violent pushing, the frenzy of pauses when I hear the raindrop sounds... how it leaps in my mouth, Henry. Oh, Henry, I can't bear to be writing you – I want you desperately, I want to open my legs so wide, I'm melting and palpitating. I want to do things so wild with you that I don't know how to say them.

ANAÏS NIN (1903-1977), TO HENRY MILLER

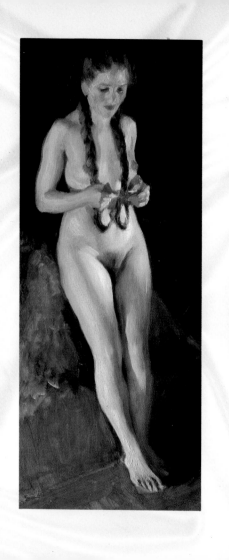

So this was what it was like. This was that thing they called passion, that had lurked in music and made her cry, and had flashed out of poetry and made her quiver – at long intervals, at long, long intervals in the sunny, empty years that had been her life. Now it had got her; and was it pain or joy? Why, it was joy. But joy so acute, so excessive, that the least touch would turn it into agony, a heaven so perfect that the least flaw, the least shadow, would ruin it into hell.

ELIZABETH VON ARNIM (1866-1941), FROM *"LOVE"*

There can be no happiness greater than I enjoyed this afternoon with you, clasped in your arms, your voice mingling with mine, your eyes in mine, your heart upon my heart, our very souls welded together. For me, there is no man on this earth but you. The others I perceive only through your love. I enjoy nothing without you.... I need your kisses upon my lips, your love in my soul.

JULIETTE DROUET, TO VICTOR HUGO

*H*e took her in his arms again and drew
her to him, and suddenly she became
small in his arms, small and nestling.
It was gone, the resistance was gone,
and she began to melt in a marvellous
peace. And as she melted small and
wonderful in his arms, she became
infinitely desirable to him, all his
blood-vessels seemed to scald with
intense yet tender desire, for her, for
her softness, for the penetrating beauty
of her in his arms, passing into his
blood. And softly, with that marvellous
swoon-like caress of his hand in pure
soft desire, softly he stroked the silky
slope of her loins, down, down between
her soft warm buttocks, coming nearer
and nearer to the very quick of her.
And she felt him like a flame of desire,
yet tender, and she felt herself melting
in the flame. She let herself go. She
felt his penis risen against her with

silent amazing force and assertion, and she let herself go to him. She yielded with a quiver that was like death, she went all open to him. And oh, if he

were not tender to her now, how cruel, for she was all open to him and helpless!

D. H. LAWRENCE (1885-1930),
FROM "LADY CHATTERLEY'S LOVER"

*H*is mouth wandered, wandered, almost touched her ear. She felt the first deep flame run over her.... He had found the soft down that lay back beyond her

cheeks, near the roots of her ears. And his mouth stirred it delicately, as infernal angels stir the fires with glass rods....

D. H. LAWRENCE (1885-1930), FROM *"MR NOON"*

Leisurely, with infinite care, he bestowed on her the finesse of a lifetime, kisses meant to entice, to mesmerize, to tap every sensual impulse she possessed. Her arms were already encircling his neck when his tongue seduced her lips to part, entered, and took her swiftly to that realm of not-caring-what-he did.

JOHANNA LINDSEY, FROM "GENTLE ROGUE"

To kiss well one must kiss solely... passion is sweeter split strand by strand.

JEANETTE WINTERSON, b. 1959

The joints of thy thighs are like jewels, the work
of the hands of a cunning workman.
Thy navel is like a round goblet, which wanteth
not liquor: thy belly is like an heap of wheat set
about with lilies.
Thy two breasts are like two young roes
that are twins....
How fair and how pleasant art thou,
O love, for delights!
This thy stature is like to a palm tree, and
thy breasts to clusters of grapes.
I said, I will go up to the palm tree, I will take
hold of the boughs thereof: now also thy
breasts shall be as clusters of the vine, and the
smell of thy nose like apples;
And the roof of thy mouth like the best wine for
my beloved, that goeth down sweetly, causing the
lips of those that are asleep to speak.
I am my beloved's, and his delight is toward me.

SONG OF SOLOMON

THE CRY OF MY BODY FOR COMPLETENESS,

THAT IS A CRY TO YOU.

MARY CAROLYN DAVIES

MUSIC! WITH YOU, TOUCHING MY FINGER-TIPS!

MUSIC! WITH YOU, SOUL ON YOUR PARTED LIPS!

MUSIC – IS YOU!

ALICE DUNBAR NELSON (1875-1935)

I HAVE SEEN ONLY YOU,

I HAVE ADMIRED ONLY YOU,

I DESIRE ONLY YOU.

NAPOLEON BONAPARTE (1769-1821)

I long to lie restingly in your flesh, with your strong protecting limbs around me, drinking in your breath, tickled by your small hands of love and by your hair, made crazy by your flaming mouth.

I long to lie with my body heavy on top of your breasts and face, to grasp your legs with my hands, to discover the way there between your legs through all the hair with my mouth and suck there lovingly in the soft barbaric flesh, there where thousands of years of

civilisation end, where the power of nationality disappears, & where blended God, Brute, & Savage writhe in ecstasy & agony. The flesh there cannot be covered, the smell of sex cannot be entirely washed away, uncontrolled movements there twitch & quiver, spasms lurk, blind devil-gods lash wild-willing horses there within; in lowness, selfishness, and greediness there slumber lazily the highest gods.

PERCY GRAINGER (1882-1961) TO KAREN HOLTEN

*B*ecause she was not of his world, because she was so simple and young and headlong, adoring and defenceless, how could he be other than her protector, in the dark! Because she was all simple Nature and beauty, as much a part of this spring night as was

the living blossom, how should he

not take all that she would give

him – how not fulfil the spring in

her heart and his! And torn

between these two emotions he

clasped her close, and kissed her

hair. How long they stood there

without speaking he knew not. The

stream went on chattering, the

owls hooting, the moon kept

stealing up and growing whiter;

the blossom all round them and

above brightened in suspense of

living beauty. Their lips had

sought each other's....

JOHN GALSWORTHY (1807-1933),
FROM "THE APPLE TREE"

I BELIEVE IN THE FLESH AND THE APPETITES,

SEEING HEARING AND FEELING ARE MIRACLES, AND EACH

PART AND TAG OF ME IS A MIRACLE.

DIVINE AM I INSIDE AND OUT, AND I MAKE HOLY

WHATEVER I TOUCH OR AM TOUCHED FROM;

THE SCENT OF THESE ARM-PITS IS AROMA

FINER THAN PRAYER,

THIS HEAD IS MORE THAN CHURCHES OR

BIBLES OR CREEDS.

IF I WORSHIP ANY PARTICULAR THING IT SHALL BE SOME

OF THE SPREAD OF MY BODY...

HANDS I HAVE TAKEN, FACE I HAVE KISSED,

MORTAL I HAVE EVER

TOUCHED, IT SHALL BE YOU.

WALT WHITMAN (1819-1891),
FROM *"LEAVES OF GRASS"*

ON BEACHES WASHED BY SEAS

OLDER THAN THE EARTH

IN THE GROVES FILLED WITH

   BIRD-CRIES,

ON THE BANKS SHADED AND

CLUSTERED WITH FLOWERS,

   WHEN WE MADE LOVE

MY EYES SAW HIM

AND MY EARS HEARD HIM;

MY ARMS GROW BEAUTIFUL

IN THE COUPLING

AND GROW LEAN

AS THEY COME AWAY.

   WHAT SHALL I MAKE OF THIS?

UNKNOWN INDIAN POET, (THIRD CENTURY),
"WHAT SHE SAID TO HER GIRL-FRIEND"

I cannot wash off the scent, and every moment the thought comes across me of those mysterious recesses of beauty where my hands have been wandering, and my heart sinks with a sweet faintness and my blood tingles through every limb for a moment and then all is still again in calm joy and thankfulness to our loving God.

CHARLES KINGSLEY (1819-1875), TO HIS WIFE FANNY

When we have loved, my love,
Panting and pale from love,
Then from your cheeks, my love,
Scent of the sweat I love:
And when our bodies love
Now to relax in love
After the stress of love,
Ever still more I love
Our mingled breath of love.

FROM THE SANSKRIT

It is winter still

but this morning while

we made love the rose opened

W.S. MERWIN, FROM *"FINDING THE ISLANDS"*

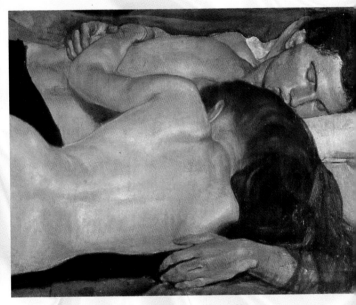

... your face after love, close to the pillow,
a lullaby.

ANNE SEXTON (1928-1974)